D0753337

To the Reader . . .

"World Cities" focuses on cities as a way to learn about the major civilizations of the world. Each civilization has at its roots the life of one or more cities. Learning about life in the great cities is essential to understanding the past and present of the world and its people.

People live in cities for many reasons. For one thing, they value what cities can offer them culturally. Culture thrives in all cities. It is expressed in visual arts, music, and ethnic celebrations. In fact, a city's greatness is often measured by the richness of culture that it offers those who live there.

Many people choose to live in cities for economic reasons. Cities offer a variety of jobs and other economic opportunities. Many city dwellers have found prosperity through trade. Nearly all the world's great cities were founded on trade—the voluntary exchange of goods and services between people. The great cities remain major economic centers.

City living can, of course, have its disadvantages. Despite these disadvantages, cities continue to thrive. By reading about the people, culture, geography, and economy of various metropolitan centers, you will understand why. You will also understand why the world is becoming more and more urban. Finally, you will learn what it is that makes each world city unique.

Mark Schug, Consulting Editor
Co-author of *Teaching Social Studies in the Elementary School* and *Community Study*

CONSULTING EDITOR
Mark C. Schug
Professor of Curriculum and Instruction
University of Wisconsin-Milwaukee

EDITORIAL
Amy Bauman, Project Editor
Barbara J. Behm
Judith Smart, Editor-in-Chief

ART/PRODUCTION
Suzanne Beck, Art Director
Carole Kramer, Designer
Thom Pharmakis, Photo Researcher
Eileen Rickey, Typesetter
Andrew Rupniewski, Production Manager

Reviewed for accuracy by:
Irwin Rubin
Joint Council on Economic Education
New York, New York   .

"Stars" © 1947 by Langston Hughes. Reprinted from *Selected Poems of Langston Hughes,* by permission of Alfred A. Knopf, Inc.

Quoted material on page 39 from Sophia Kreitzberg, © *Seaport* magazine 1986, South Street Seaport Museum.

Library of Congress Number: 89-10466

1 2 3 4 5 6 7 8 9   93 92 91 90 89

Library of Congress Cataloging in Publication Data

Davis, Jim, 1940-
  New York City.
  (World cities)

  Summary: Explores the history, cultural heritage, demographics, geography, and economic and natural resources of New York City.
  1. New York (N.Y.)—Juvenile literature. [1. New York (N.Y.)] I. Hawke, Sharryl Davis. II. Title. III. Series: Davis, Jim, 1940- . World cities.
  F128.33.D38 1989   974.7'1   [B] [92]   89-10466
  ISBN 0-8172-3031-9 (lib. bdg.)

**Cover Photo: Pete Fedynich, Jr./
            Jeff Greenberg, Photo Agent**

NEW YORK CITY

WORLD CITIES

JAMES E. DAVIS
AND
SHARRYL DAVIS HAWKE

RAINTREE PUBLISHERS
Milwaukee

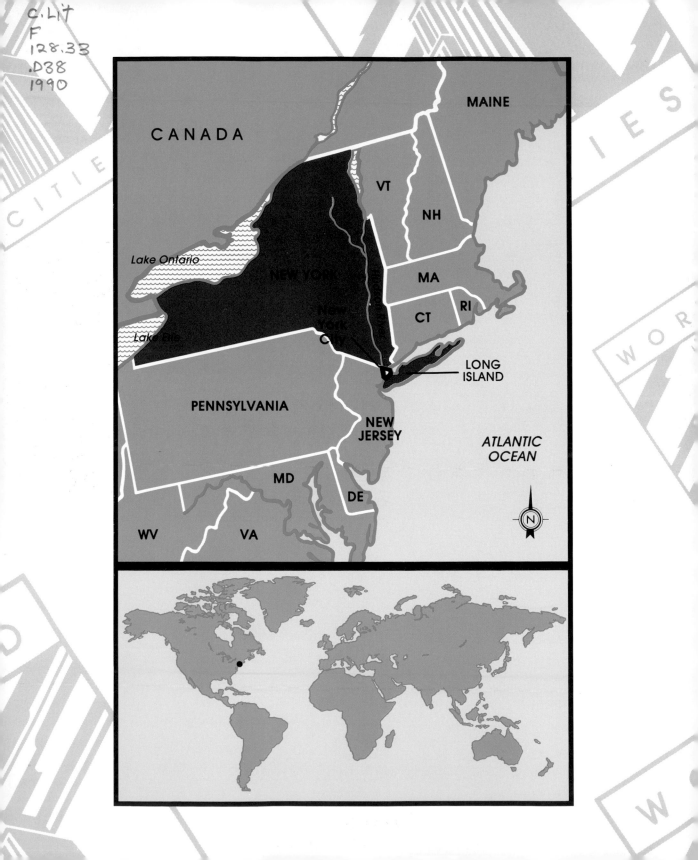

CANADA

MAINE

VT

NH

Lake Ontario

NEW YORK

MA

New York City

CT

RI

LONG ISLAND

PENNSYLVANIA

NEW JERSEY

ATLANTIC OCEAN

Lake Erie

MD

DE

WV

VA

N

Contents

New York State Department of Economic Development

Introduction

What do you think of when you think of New York City? Skyscrapers? Subways? Street gangs? Broadway? Times Square on New Year's Eve? The Statue of Liberty? The Empire State Building? New York is all of these things and much more.

If you look at New York on a map, you will see a coastal city that includes islands. The Atlantic Ocean, New York Bay, and deep river waterways wind between parts of New York City. It is these deep waterways and the city's location on the Atlantic Ocean that have made New York a busy shipping port and an important world city.

The islands and coastal areas make up the five boroughs of New York City. A borough is a separate area or region. Manhattan is the main borough. It is connected by bridge, tunnel, and ferry to the other four boroughs, which are Brooklyn, the Bronx, Queens, and Staten Island. Only the Bronx touches the mainland of the United States.

A Visit to New York

When you walk down a street in New York City, you walk in the shadows of the city's many tall buildings. Millions of years ago, glaciers carved this land down to solid rock. Without such a sturdy base, it would have been impossible to build the huge skyscrapers that form the city's skyline. In New York, you find street after street

A view of Manhattan shows the waterways that have made New York an important seaport.

of skyscrapers. All of them are very close together. The sounds of the street echo from the sides of these huge buildings and fill the air—horns honking, cars moving, vendors calling out. If you look up as you walk along, the sight of the buildings reaching so far above your head will almost make you dizzy.

The sidewalks are crowded with people bustling along. Over seven million people live in New York City. If you can hear above the noise, you will hear people speaking different languages. You will also hear people speaking English with many different accents. The smell of the food from sidewalk vendors will also attract your attention.

There is so much to see in New York. In the borough of Manhattan, you can visit the Empire State Building, Central Park, and many museums. You can see Broadway plays, ride the subways, or look out from the top of the tallest skyscrapers in New York—the twin towers of the World Trade Center. New York is the country's number one city for entertainment. Jazz musicians from southern and midwestern states nicknamed New York City the "Big Apple" because they said to perform there meant you had made it to the top.

New York in the Early Days

During the early days of this country, New York City became a center for making clothing, or garments. Some of the first garments made in New York were uniforms for the young country's army. Today, the garment industry is still a major New York business.

At the same time as the city was developing a garment industry, it was becoming a center of finance. Finance is the business of money. One part of the finance business is banks. Banks hold people's money on deposit, and they make loans to people and businesses. Many important banks are in New York City.

Another part of finance is called the stock market. Individuals own shares of corporations, or businesses. The shares of ownership are called stock. Stocks are pieces of paper and people buy and sell them. To set up the rules for how people should buy and sell stock, business people in New York get together on Wall Street to decide what the rules should be. Today, Wall Street is a world center for banking and stock trading.

Nearly two hundred years ago, New York suffered a great fire. It took a long time for the city to recover from the fire, but it did. New York's Atlantic coast location helped it recover because the city could continue its busy shipping industry. From its beginning, New York was an important shipping port. From there, furs and wheat were exported to Europe. In return, goods the colonists needed were imported to the United States through this port.

Immigration Begins

When people move from one country to another, they are called immigrants. The year 1840 marked the beginning of a great wave of people moving from Europe to the United States. Many of the immigrants came through New York City. In fifteen years, the population of the city doubled. At one time, government officials decided that all immigrants to this country who came through New York would land first on Ellis Island in New York Bay.

The population of New York continued to grow rapidly until World War I. All these people needed housing and ways to get around. So New Yorkers built small apartment houses,

New York's sidewalks overflow with people headed for various destinations.

Carlye Calvin

Many New Yorkers settle into neighborhoods with others who share their heritage. Above, a fruit-seller tends his Chinatown market.

subways, and railways. Business grew quickly on the island of Manhattan. Since the island is only 12 miles (19 kilometers) long and 2.5 miles (4 km) wide, New Yorkers soon ran out of land for their homes and businesses. But the people of New York found a solution to this problem in skyscrapers. Some skyscrapers are over one hundred stories tall. They really "scrape the sky." Today, small skyscrapers are sometimes torn down to make room for even taller skyscrapers.

A City of Ethnic Groups

New York is a bustling city of many races and people from many different countries. Greek, Irish, German, Black, Puerto Rican, Chinese, and other ethnic groups have their own communities in New York. The great differences among these groups make New York a lively city. At the same time, the groups sometimes come into conflict.

Conflict has been a part of New York life since the city's beginning. In fact, how the city has been able to resolve conflicts among its ethnic groups is an important part of the New York story. By finding ways to use the backgrounds and abilities of its residents, New York has grown into a leading world city.

WORLD CITIES

How the City Began

Have you ever thought about what it would be like to live in the past? Your parents remember when there were no VCRs (videocassette recorders) or microwave ovens. When they were your age, they didn't play computer games or fasten their shoes with Velcro. Your grandparents probably remember playing with yoyos and listening to radio "soap operas" in the days before television. What about life long, long ago? What was it like to live in the area that is now New York City? How did the city begin?

Indians Were the First New Yorkers

The first people to live on the land that became New York were Indians.

They came to the island of Manhattan about three thousand years ago. They called the place *Manhatta,* which is an Indian word for "hilly island." The Indians lived in caves or bark huts. They hunted and trapped animals. They fished, collected berries, and later grew crops. If it weren't for the Indians, you might never have eaten corn. It was the Indians who taught early white settlers how to grow corn.

Indian children didn't go to schools like those of today. But they had to learn many things before they grew up. Boys had to learn to imitate animal sounds to become good hunters. They also learned how to take the poison from a rattlesnake. They dipped their arrowheads in the poison and then used them for hunting. Girls learned to cook and tend crops.

Many of the early Indian paths are city streets today. The Indian paths led to fields of berries, beaver traps, or favorite fishing spots. Today, those paths may lead to schools, libraries, businesses, and beaches.

Explorers Come to the New World

An Italian explorer named Giovanni da Verrazano was the first white person to see the area. He sailed a French ship into New York Bay in 1524. When a storm came up, he left the bay quickly. The Verrazano-Narrows Bridge is named after him. It connects the borough of Staten Island with the borough of Brooklyn.

In 1609, Henry Hudson came from England to this new land. He made his way inland on the river, which was named Hudson for him. He worked for the Dutch East India Company of Holland. Hudson, who was looking for a waterway to Asia, stopped to explore the area around New York. He met the Indians who lived there. The Indians thought he was afraid of them, so they threw their arrows into a fire to show they wouldn't harm him. He bought beaver skins, called pelts, and fur from the Indians.

When Hudson returned to Holland, the Dutch claimed the land he discov-

ered. He told them it was the richest farmland he had ever seen. He showed them the beaver pelts. The Dutch were eager to buy beaver pelts. They could make a lot of money selling them in Europe. Beaver pelts were used to make hats that were very popular at that time.

A Colony Is Formed

Dutch merchants formed the Dutch West India Company in 1621. They sent people to the New World to set up a colony. These people were called settlers or colonists. They settled on the eastern tip of the island of Manhattan and called it New Amsterdam. They called the surrounding area New Netherland.

The early settlers traded with the Indians. They traded trinkets for the

The J. Clarence Davies Collection, Museum of the City of New York

This view of New Amsterdam shows the windmills and wooden houses built by Dutch settlers.

Indians' beaver pelts, which they then shipped to Holland. Soon the Dutch West India Company was selling beaver pelts to all of Europe.

Peter Minuit was made governor of the colony for the Dutch West India Company. In 1626, he bought the island of Manhattan from the Indians for some cloth and beads. Some people think Minuit tricked the Indians.

Early Days in the Colony

As the white people came to the New World, the Indians' way of life changed. The settlers cut down the forests where the Indians hunted. Fur trappers competed with the Indians for game and beaver pelts. These changes caused conflicts between the settlers and the Indians. The conflicts often led to battles.

By the late 1600s, the colonists had forced most of the Indians to leave the New Amsterdam area. A tall wooden wall was built to keep the Indians out. It went across the island of Manhattan from the Hudson River to the East River. The wall didn't work very well though. Settlers pulled off chunks of it to use as firewood. In 1699, the British tore down the wall. They made a street where the wall had been. Today, this street is the famous Wall Street.

There were about eight hundred white settlers in the colony by 1643. Most of them came from Holland, but many were not Dutch. Many of these settlers were people who had gone to Holland from other countries. They had felt unwelcome in their homelands because of their religious beliefs. So they first went to Holland and then came to the New World seeking religious freedom. The hope of religious freedom attracted many people to the New World. There were as many as eighteen languages spoken in the new colony. Today, New York is still a city of people with many different backgrounds and faiths.

Life for the First Settlers

Life was not easy for the early white settlers. Food was scarce. The houses were built of wood, including the chimneys. There were frequent fires.

The settlers' houses looked very much like the houses in Holland looked at that time. They had steep roofs and Dutch doors. With Dutch doors, the top part of the door was opened to let in fresh air and light. The bottom part could remain closed to keep the animals from coming into the house. Outside the house was an outhouse, or outdoor toilet. Each house had to provide its own water. Some people had barrels for catching rain. Others dug wells. The settlers also built windmills.

Whenever the settlers dug foundations for their homes and buildings, they hauled the dirt to the rivers. By filling in part of the rivers, they made more land. This practice began in Holland and continues in New York today.

Most city streets were just beaten paths. Few had names. Someone wanting directions might be told, "Follow the path that goes from Jan Dyke's house to the pond." Also, the city streets were filthy. Pigs, goats, cows, and dogs roamed everywhere. They sometimes trampled gardens. The settlers dug a canal so they could travel in boats, like they had in Holland. Many people threw their garbage in the canal, and it became polluted. Finally, they filled the canal with dirt and made it a road. Today, this road is Broad Street.

Good farmland was plentiful here. Many English people moved from other colonies to work the farmland of New Netherland. Slaves were brought from the West Indies to work on the farms. Some Indians were also used as slaves. The English called Dutch settlers Jan-Kees. *Jan* was a common Dutch name. *Kees* was Dutch for "cheese," a popular Dutch food. "Jan-Kees" became "Yankees" during the American Revolutionary War.

Many other people in the small city were shopkeepers. They sold goods and supplies to the farmers. The early merchants had shops in their homes. These homes they called double houses. The shop was in the front of the house. The family lived in back. The second floor was a warehouse.

Today, New York is still a city of many shops, but these shops have changed over the years.

A Dutch immigrant named Peter Stuyvesant was made governor of the colony in 1647. He set up fire regulations, started a hospital, and opened a post office. He also ordered taverns to close at 9:00 P.M. Even though he was not a popular leader, the colony prospered. The Stuyvesant neighborhood in Brooklyn was named for him.

British Claim the Colony

In 1664, the British took over the colony without a battle. With four warships, the British sailed into the harbor and demanded that the Dutch leaders give up their colony. The colonists could not defend themselves. They had very little ammunition. Besides, many colonists felt no loyalty to the Dutch. The colony now belonged to the British, who renamed the colony New York. Nine years later, the

Dutch settlers plead with Governor Stuyvesant not to surrender New Amsterdam to the attacking British forces.

Dutch navy took the colony back. They called it New Orange. But before long, the British took control again.

The city grew in an orderly way under the British. There was a shipping area, a business district, a warehouse area, and a manufacturing district. The smelly businesses of animal slaughter and tanning were kept on the edge of town. The British made English the official language. Many adults who were not British didn't bother to learn this new language. But their children learned it. They spoke English when they were with other children and at school. They spoke their parents' language at home.

Some of the early settlers who did not like the British people moved to a small settlement in New Harlem. Since there were no roads in Harlem, people had to travel by canoe each Sunday to go to church in New York.

Meanwhile, merchants needed more land to build their shops in the central part of the city. They bought land in the East River and filled it in with dirt. This area became a new business district called Water Street.

The Colonists Want Freedom

Many people did not like British rule. They wanted the freedom to govern themselves. In 1774, a group called the Sons of Liberty struck a blow for independence. The Sons of Liberty were against the high taxes they had to pay to England. In Boston a year earlier, a high tax on imported tea had angered the colonists. In protest, the Boston colonists raided British cargo ships, dressed as Indians. They dumped the entire cargo of tea into the Boston Harbor. This incident became known as the Boston Tea Party. Following this example, the Sons of Liberty held a "tea party" of their own. They boarded the next British ship and dumped its cargo of tea into the New York harbor.

John Peter Zenger was an immigrant from Germany. As a colonist in New York, he published a newspaper called the *New York Weekly Journal*. In it, Zenger often printed articles that criticized the British government, particularly New York's governor, William Cosby. When Cosby demanded to know who had written the critical articles, Zenger refused to say. Zenger was arrested and accused of libel. Libel is a statement, whether written or printed, that is damaging to another's reputation. In jail, Zenger continued his work. He was backed by some powerful people who opposed Cosby's government. They, too, thought that Zenger should have the freedom to print even critical articles about the British. Andrew Hamilton, a famous attorney, defended Zenger.

Federal Hall, seen here, was the first United States Capitol. Shown in the etching is the 1789 inauguration of George Washington.

He argued that what Zenger had printed was true. If it was true, Zenger could not be guilty of libel. Hamilton's words, which focused on the idea of liberty, convinced the jury to vote "not guilty." Zenger's trial became an important event in favor of freedom of the press.

The Revolutionary War began in 1776. The war was fought between the American colonists and the British. The Americans wanted to be free from British rule. New York was important during the war for three reasons. First, it was located at about the center of the fighting. Second, because of its location on major waterways, troops and supplies could be easily moved in and out of the city. Third, the merchants and leaders of New York were angry about the British taxes and supported the revolution.

In 1783, the colonists won the war. The colonists were now free from British rule. But soon after the end of the war, New Yorkers faced another challenge. A great fire destroyed one-fourth of the city. Between the war and the great fire, the city was in ruins. It was time to rebuild, and New York did rebuild. It became the capital of the new nation. George Washington was inaugurated in New York as the first president of the United States on April 30, 1789.

CHAPTER 2

WORLD CITIES

Growth of the City to 1900

After the Revolutionary War, Americans were determined to rebuild the new country. People were filled with excitement and pride. Americans had the promise of freedom and the hope for a strong future.

The Beginnings of Wall Street

Congress needed to sell bonds to pay back money borrowed during the Revolutionary War. Investors did not want to buy the bonds because they didn't have a way to sell them later. So a group of businesspeople met in the shade of a buttonwood tree to set up rules for buying and selling bonds and stocks. As this area developed, it became the center for stock exchange and banking. The place is now known as Wall Street. This famous street, as you may remember, was named for the wall that the settlers had erected there in the 1600s. Today, although the buttonwood tree still grows there, businesspeople now meet in the stock brokerage houses and in the New York Stock Exchange buildings.

Problems of a Growing City

The water supply was a major problem of the growing city. Most people got their water from Collect Pond. It was located near present-day Centre Street. The water was so foul that even the horses refused to drink it. People who could afford to buy their drinking water got their water from privately owned pumps or springs. Because of the poor water and filthy streets, there was much sickness. Many people died of yellow fever and smallpox. Some people moved out of the city. They fled to the countryside of New Harlem.

Still, nothing was done about the city's water until after the fire of 1835. The fire covered 20 acres (8 hectares) and destroyed 674 buildings. Afterward, the city needed both new buildings and a water supply. In 1842, the Croton Aqueduct was completed. An aqueduct is a system of pipes designed to carry water. It carried water from the Croton Reservoir to homes many miles away. It supplied water for six thousand homes. It also provided for the city's first fire hydrants.

Clean water helped, but it was not enough to stop disease in a city growing more crowded. Immigrants continued to pour in from Europe. Between 1820 and 1860, the population grew from 161,000 to 814,000. Many people were poor, and there were not enough homes for everyone.

Many people lived together in small apartments called tenements. The crowding, along with little light or fresh air, made the apartments unhealthy. This was especially true during the hot summer months. Many people died as a result of unhealthy conditions. In his book *How the Other Half Lives,* writer Jacob Riis describes the

Pipe laid for a section of the Croton Aqueduct runs through Central Park.

terrible living conditions in New York tenements that sometimes drove women to abandon their infant children:

> In midwinter, when the poor shiver in their homes, and in the dog days when the fierce heat and foul air of the tenements smother their babies by thousands, they are found, sometimes three and four in a night, in hallways in areas and on the doorsteps of the rich. . . .

Transportation

Transportation is always a problem for a large and crowded city. New York was no different. Bicycles became the most popular form of personal transportation. The bicycle also made it acceptable for women to wear pants.

In 1881, New Yorkers flocked to the Central Park Zoo to view some of the first hippopotamuses ever brought to the United States.

The pants were called pedal pushers. There were even bicycles that entire families could ride. The children sat in the middle while the adults pedaled.

The first elevated railroad was built in 1878. An elevated railroad ran on tracks set on posts that rose above the city streets. In 1899, electric streetcars rushed noisily for many blocks in Manhattan. The streetcars were connected to electric wires strung from poles above the streets. In 1904, the first subway in Manhattan was opened. A subway is a train that runs in underground tunnels.

Entertainment

When they could manage a treat for themselves, people sought various kinds of entertainment. Wild-animal shows were popular. One show had the first hippopotamus ever seen in the United States. A popular attraction was "The Living Happy Family." This "happy family" was a collection of animals that are natural enemies such as cats and rats, owls and mice, and eagles and rabbits. These animals had been trained to live together peaceably.

Central Park, located in the middle of Manhattan island, was built in the mid-1800s. Its splendor attracted the city's rich and fashionable people. Every afternoon, these people had a carriage parade. They dressed in their finest clothes and showed off their carriages. Sometimes daring women even drove the horse-drawn carriages.

When people began building railroads, Coney Island was developed as a resort. Coney Island became a famous seaside resort, with its long public beach and amusements. Visitors took the Fulton Ferry from Manhattan to Brooklyn. From there, they took the train to Coney Island. Before people settled in the area, Coney Island had been an Indian hunting ground.

Coney Island had over sixty hotels, three amusement parks, racetracks, saloons, restaurants, and beaches. And, of course, hot dogs were served. Today, amusement parks all over the country serve Coney Dogs—hot dogs with chili or pickle relish—which were named for Coney Island. By the mid-1800s, railroads linked most parts of Manhattan, and Harlem, on the north end, grew as a summer resort area. During the late 1800s, many people began to move there to live. Construction in Harlem boomed.

During the 1880s, city dwellers rode in light horse carts on Sunday outings to resort areas like Coney Island.

Early Working Conditions

Working conditions in the late 1800s were generally poor. One of the major industries was the garmet-making industry. Many people, mostly women, worked in clothing manufacturing shops. These shops were called sweatshops because they were hot, miserable places. People sweated, working long hours for little pay.

New York was a great seaport, and there were many sailors. Boys often left home at an early age to go to sea. Children as young as eight years old served as cabin boys. When their ships sailed from port, they might not return home for several years.

Most children had to work to help their families. Some worked on their families' farms. Some children in town worked as apprentices. An apprentice worked for a craftsman, learning a trade such as carpentry. In exchange for learning the trade, an apprentice had to work for the master craftsman until the age of twenty-one.

Some children worked as peddlers. They carried baskets of fruits or vegetables throughout neighborhoods. They shouted rhymed street cries to announce their coming to the housewives who bought from them. A cherry peddler would call out,

Cherries! Cherries! Cherries!
Here's Cherries!

Do you want any cherries,
Just picked from the tree
Black, Ox-heart, or Red,
As fine as can be!

Adults also sold their goods door-to-door. They were called vendors. Since there were no cars, people didn't go out to shop very often. They depended on the deliverymen such as the milkman who delivered milk and the iceman who delivered ice.

Tammany Hall

Tammany Hall was the name given to a group of people who tried to change some of New York's early laws. This group was powerful in New York for over 140 years, from 1801 to 1943. Tammany Hall members were successful in getting the New York legislature to allow immigrants to vote. They also pushed for laws to help the working people. To do this, the members of Tammany Hall challenged the power of the landowners. They fought against a rule that said only people who owned property could vote.

In return, Tammany leaders expected certain favors. For example, those who were helped were expected to vote for Tammany Hall candidates. Other people who wanted jobs had to give money to support these Tammany candidates. This is called patronage. Some say the patronage system is still used today in New York City, even though it is not legal.

Some people misused the power of Tammany Hall. One of those people was William Tweed. Tweed was called "Boss Tweed," and he was a leader of Tammany Hall between 1852 and 1870. It is estimated that Tweed and his partners cheated the city government out of between $30 million and $200 million.

Other Important New Yorkers

During the 1800s, New York struggled with the problems and excitement of a growing city. Many individuals and groups of people contributed ideas to help the city through its growing pains.

De Witt Clinton was a famous mayor of New York City. He was mayor for all but one year between 1803 and 1815. He later became the governor of New York State. Clinton is well known as the man who promoted the building of the Erie Canal. Clinton understood that the canal would encourage trade. Trade, in turn, would create wealth for the city.

This canal connects Lake Erie with the Hudson River. New Yorkers celebrated the opening of the canal because it was important for shipping and other business. With it, farm products and manufactured goods could

Sweatshops often employed very young children and forced them to work long hours for little pay.

easily be moved from the Great Lakes area all the way to the Atlantic Ocean. Many towns grew up along the canal. Without a doubt, this waterway contributed to New York City's rapid growth as the nation's leading seaport.

It took eight years to build the canal. Work began in 1817 and was completed in 1825. Many of the workers on the Erie Canal were Irish immigrants. Tammany Hall members helped some of these immigrants get jobs building the canal. It was hard work. They worked waist-deep in mud and water, with the hot sun and mosquitoes for company.

Some workers on the canal and those in the shipping ports sang songs as they worked. The song "The Erie Canal" became famous. The mule who works in the song was one of the mules or horses that walked the towpaths on the banks of the canal, pulling the small boats along.

The Erie Canal
I've got a mule, her name is Sal,
Fifteen miles on the Erie Canal.
She's a good old worker and a good old pal,
Fifteen miles on the Erie Canal.
We've haul'd some barges in our day,
Fill'd with lumber, coal, and hay,
And we know ev'ry inch of the way
From Albany to Buffalo.

Low bridge, ev'rybody down!
Low bridge, for we're going through a town,
And you'll always know your neighbor,
You'll always know your pal,
If you ever navigated on the Erie Canal.

Another interesting New Yorker was John Randel. Randel's work has affected the lives of New Yorkers since 1811. Randel designed the street plan for Manhattan. His plan fixed the location for future homes and businesses. Most of the area was open countryside when Randel laid out his plan to organize the city into rectangular blocks. The Randel Plan went from Fourteenth Street north to Harlem.

Federick Law Olmstead was another important New York designer. Olmstead designed parks and dreamed of building a park in Manhattan. On the land he selected, stood a shantytown. A shantytown is a group of shacks where poor people live. The shantytown residents were forced to leave. Work on Olmstead's park began in 1857 and took twenty years to complete. This park was named Central Park. It is located between 59th and 110th Streets in Manhattan.

John Roebling dreamed of building a bridge to connect Brooklyn and Manhattan. He never saw the bridge built, but his son Washington Roebling took over his dream. Washington Roebling engineered the bridge that became the famous Brooklyn Bridge. It took fourteen years—from 1870 to 1883—to build it. It was dangerous work because men had to work in tunnels under the water. More than twenty men died building the bridge.

The Brooklyn Bridge is 1,595 feet (486 meters) long. It was the world's longest bridge when it was completed. At that time, it was considered one of the engineering wonders of the world. The bridge not only linked Brooklyn to the island of Manhattan; it also linked businesses and people. Today, a lively Manhattan depends on the bridges and tunnels that cross the rivers bringing people and products to and from the island.

Another important New Yorker was a Catholic nun, Mother Elizabeth Seton. She helped start the Catholic schools in America. The first was in 1809. She also founded the first order of nuns in this country. The nuns were called the American Sisters of Charity. The Catholic Church made Mother Seton the first American saint.

During the building of the Brooklyn Bridge, strolls along the catwalks used by workers became a popular evening pastime.

WORLD

CITIES

New York in the Twentieth Century

New York City's population grew rapidly until more recent times. The table below shows the city's population in selected years. Notice the large population increase between 1860 and 1940.

Chart Design: Eileen Rickey

New York City Population, Selected Years*	
1700	5,000
1775	25,000
1820	161,000
1860	814,000
1900	3,437,000
1940	7,455,000
1980	7,072,000
YEAR	POPULATION

*Rounded to the nearest 1,000 (Source: U.S. Bureau of the Census)

Part of the great population increase just before 1900 resulted from joining different regions of the New York area to form Greater New York. By 1900, the population of Greater New York was more than three million. New York in the early 1900s was a city struggling with fast population growth. New Yorkers have always succeeded in working out problems that come from serving many people.

Working Conditions in the Early 1900s

In the early 1900s, New York became America's economic capital. It had almost forty thousand manufacturing companies. These were companies that made different products to

Top of page: In the garment district of nineteenth century New York, porters lug newly made clothing. Today, workers use wheeled carts (above).

sell. The top manufacturing companies produced clothing, published books and newspapers, made tools, or packaged food. These are still among the top industries in New York today. These industries were small and didn't need much space. Their location on the waterways made shipping easy.

As business grew in central and southern Manhattan, many people moved to the north side of Manhattan. Better transportation—including bridges and tunnels for cars, and a subway system—allowed people to travel greater distances to jobs. Workers came from all parts of the city and from nearby states.

People came to the city from other countries or other parts of the United States, hoping to find jobs. Many of these people were poor and looking for new opportunities. They found jobs, but the pay was often low and the work hours were long. Sometimes the working conditions were not safe.

Many women and children worked in poor conditions in the garment-making industry. A horrible fire at the Triangle Waist Company killed many workers. This accident brought about some changes to the industry. Workers had begun to organize themselves into groups called unions. Through unions, people were able to fight for better working conditions and better pay. The first industries in New York to have unions were the printing and metalworking industries.

Wall Street Was Important

The Wall Street area was growing in importance in money and banking. People who worked there were making financial decisions that affected the United States and other parts of the world.

Many Wall Street bankers became rich and powerful. One of the most famous was J.P. Morgan. He was a very successful banker and powerful investor in the stock market. When he died in 1913, he left his son four banks, three trust companies, three insurance companies, ten railroads, three streetcar companies, and many other small companies.

A New Idea—Skyscrapers

Two inventions of the late 1800s made skyscrapers possible. One was the invention of the steel frame by the American architect William Le Baron Jenney. Jenney developed a steel frame that could support thousands of tons of stone and concrete. The idea for the frame came to Jenney when his wife accidentally dropped a heavy book on a bird cage. He noticed it didn't damage the cage. By the early 1900s, skyscrapers were changing the city's skyline. The skyscrapers were so sturdy that when an aircraft crashed into the

Empire State Building in 1945, it merely tore a hole in the building.

The second invention important to skyscrapers was the elevator. Passenger elevators were developed by Elisha G. Otis in 1854. Otis's elevator had an automatic safety device that kept the elevator from falling even if the cable broke. This device made the elevator safe for passengers, and the first was installed in New York City in 1857. The Otis Company still makes elevators. Look for the company's name next time you ride in an elevator.

Life in the City Improves

When Greater New York was formed, people began working in official groups to help with city planning.

The Metropolitan Museum of Art (below) houses collections of art from every part of the world.

New York Convention & Visitors Bureau

These groups helped plan for future neighborhoods, businesses, and city streets. They also formed an arts commission.

Interest in the arts and sciences increased in the early 1900s. Three New Yorkers contributed to the building and support of one of New York's major public libraries. They were John J. Astor, James Lenox, and Samuel Tilden. Money from another famous New Yorker, Andrew Carnegie, provided the city with sixty-two branches of the main library. Carnegie also donated money to build a center for music called Carnegie Hall. Other New Yorkers helped support the American Museum of Natural History. Citizens also helped pay for the Metropolitan Museum of Art, which opened in 1902.

There were three large newspapers in New York at the time: William Randolph Hearst's *Journal,* Joseph Pulitzer's *World,* and the *New York Times.* Hearst is still a prominent name in newspaper publishing. Pulitzer founded the important Pulitzer Prizes awarded each year to writers and publishers. The *New York Times* is one of the leading newspapers in the world today.

The early 1900s was a time of growth and excitement in music and theater. The Metropolitan Opera House opened. The world's greatest soloists and orchestras performed in Carnegie Hall. The Theater District at Broadway and Forty-second Street was developing fast. Greenwich Village, a section of New York, was growing as an art, literature, and theater center. Cheap rents and a charming village atmosphere drew intellectuals and artists to the Village. They gathered in coffeehouses, taverns, restaurants, and bookstores. Some of these people became known for their "Bohemian" life-style, or free-and-easy manner. Eugene O'Neill, a famous playwright, was one of the many artists who lived there.

Built in 1891, Carnegie Hall was for many years the home of the New York Philharmonic Orchestra.

Museums like the Guggenheim (above) and the miles of fabulous shopping (below) attract thousands of visitors to New York each year.

Transportation

Transportation got a big boost in the 1900s when the first subway system was constructed in Manhattan. Three more bridges were built over the East River, connecting Manhattan to Brooklyn and Queens. A tunnel was constructed under the Hudson River. This tunnel was called "The Tube." It became the first connection between New York City and New Jersey. Another tunnel was constructed under the East River to link Brooklyn with Manhattan.

Because many more trains were coming into Manhattan, two new train stations were built. The Pennsylvania Terminal was built in 1910, and Grand Central Station was built in 1913. Today, these stations are still major centers for the Manhattan transportation system.

The 1920s

From 1914 to 1919, during World War I, the city's growth slowed down. Then New York experienced the Roaring Twenties, as the 1920s were called. The Roaring Twenties were years of growth and change. By this time, many of New York's department stores had been built and were becoming famous throughout the country. Much of the clothing they sold was made in New York City. Fifth Avenue became known worldwide as one of the most fashionable places to shop. The subway system was larger, covering more miles. And it was the age of the automobile—cars were everywhere.

Harlem continued to grow throughout the 1920s. Blacks began living in the early 1900s. By 1920, Harlem was an important black community. Its intellectuals and artists were known and respected throughout the country. This time of achievement and pride is known as the Harlem Renaissance. Harlem was an intellectual and artistic center throughout the 1930s, in spite of the poverty and crowding there. Political leader W.E.B. Du Bois and writers Langston Hughes and Richard Wright were all part of the Harlem Renaissance. Langston Hughes wrote the following poem about Harlem:

Stars
O, sweep of stars over Harlem
    Streets,
O, little breath of oblivion that is
    night.
    A city building
    To a mother's song.
    A city dreaming
    To a lullaby.
Reach up your hand, dark boy,
    and take a star.
Out of the little breath of oblivion
    That is night
    Take just
    One star.

The famous *New Yorker* magazine first appeared in 1925. This magazine is still published weekly. The Museum of Modern Art was founded in 1929. It is now one of the most important art museums in the world.

Hard Times Hit New York

The stock market crash of 1929 hit New York hard. Businesses and banks lost a great deal of money. Many were forced to close. People lost their jobs and had very little money to spend. Shantytowns sprang up here and there in the city, as little communities of people with no homes gathered together. Even Central Park had its shantytowns.

This was also a time when people in government misused their power. In 1932, the state of New York investigated the city government. Mayor Jimmy Walker was asked to resign because of serious financial problems within his administration. Whether the city's problems were caused by carelessness or corruption, Walker's image had been damaged, and he resigned.

Efforts to Recover

Fiorello La Guardia was mayor from 1934 until 1945. La Guardia, who was honest and hardworking, was a very popular mayor. He helped raise money for homes for the poor, especially homes in poor neighborhoods of the Lower East Side and Harlem. More tunnels, bridges, and highways were built. An airport in the borough of Queens, built in 1939, was renamed La Guardia Field to honor the mayor.

In spite of La Guardia's efforts to help the city's poor, some areas like Harlem were becoming run down. The population grew very quickly after World War II ended in 1945, and there was not enough good housing available.

The 1950s and 1960s

In the 1950s and 1960s, New Yorkers worked hard to keep up with the needs of the growing city. To make running the country's largest city an easier job, new city departments and committees were formed, and new borough responsibilities were set up. The city made improvements in its fire department, its police department, and in its system of education.

The number of small businesses continued to increase, but the number of small manufacturers was going down. The arts and entertainment industries were growing. On the west side of Manhattan, the Lincoln Center for Performing Arts was built. The Guggenheim Museum was built on the east side. This unusual, sphere-

La Guardia Airport's traffic tower stands against the New York City skyline.

shaped art museum was designed by the famous architect Frank Lloyd Wright.

The 1970s and 1980s

In the 1970s, manufacturing companies continued to leave the city. Some big corporations began moving their headquarters to New York's suburbs. A suburb is a city or community that is outside, but near, a large city. As companies left the city, more and more buildings were left empty. Construction slowed almost to a halt. Areas such as the South Bronx were run down. Throughout the city, slum conditions spread, and crime increased.

The city's costs continued to go up,

From the collage of billboards, neon lights, and towering, modern buildings, it is clear that New York is a thriving world city.

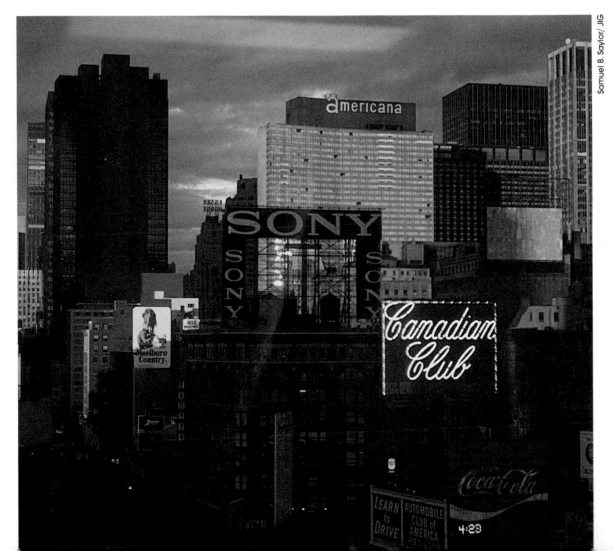

but the money it took from taxes was going down. New York was in trouble. The city even asked the United States government for help. New Yorkers began "Save New York" movements. They introduced the slogan "I Love New York" and advertised that their city was still the "Big Apple."

John Lindsay was mayor of New York City from 1966 to 1973. He gained the respect of the city's blacks and Puerto Ricans by being seen out on the streets during times of racial tension. In the mid-to-late 1970s, the mayor was Abraham Beame. He worked hard to get the budget back in shape. But he had to make large cuts that affected many people. Public hospitals were closed. Construction on public housing, libraries, and recreation centers was stopped. Many services for the people had to end, and many public employees lost their jobs.

With these cuts in city spending, and with New Yorkers' strong determination, slowly things began to get better again. Because so many offices were empty, office space became cheaper to rent. These office spaces attracted new businesses. Foreign businesses and banks soon followed. New York was looking stronger.

Today, New York City is still an important, thriving world city. The city government still has financial worries. There are problems of crime,

Changing times have not lessened New York's importance as a financial center. Above is the New York Stock Exchange.

drugs, and the homeless. Ed Koch, who became mayor in 1977, has a difficult job to do. As in the past, New Yorkers will have to work together, and they will have to work very hard to solve their problems.

WORLD
CITIES

New York: Immigrants' First Stop

The most striking thing to remember about the history of New York is the central role the city played in the country's immigration. The United States has always been a nation of immigrants. In a way, the first settlers were the first immigrants. They came mostly from Holland and England.

Many people came to the New World in search of a better life for themselves and their families. People wanted better jobs or better land to farm. Many people, as mentioned earlier, came because their religious beliefs had made them unwelcome in their homelands. Others sought political freedom. With its seemingly boundless space, rich farmland, and plentiful jobs, America was a symbol of

hope for these people. These features, together with both political and religious freedom, spurred immigration in the 1800s.

Immigrants entering America in the 1800s and early 1900s had to enter through New York. So New York was the first city seen by many immigrants to America. Many of these people went on to other cities or smaller towns. Some went farther west to farm, and others went south for the warmer weather. But many people stayed in New York City. Life was difficult for these immigrants, too. They had to adjust to a new country with new customs and a different language. Many of these people settled in areas of the city where others from their homelands lived. These ethnic neighborhoods were a unique feature of New York in the past and still are today.

Many Europeans Come to America

Robert Fulton, a New Yorker, invented the steamboat in early 1800. The steamboat could travel faster than the old ships, and because of it, many people soon came to America. Between 1800 and 1914 an average of five thousand immigrants entered the country each day. But immigration really picked up between 1830 and 1890. In that time alone, over fifteen million people came to the United States. Immigration in this period is divided into two major waves. People of the first wave, which lasted until about 1860, are known as the old immigration. Immigrants of the second wave, which lasted from 1860 to 1890, are called the new immigration.

Although the immigrants of the 1800s represented many European countries, certain ethnic groups dominated each wave. Immigrants of the first wave came mainly from northern and western Europe. Among these people, the Germans and the Irish were the most numerous. The flow of Irish immigrants had been spurred on by the potato famine of the 1840s. People in the second wave came mainly from

New York's ethnic richness is evident in the wide range of foods available in the city.

the southern and eastern European countries. Of this wave, the Italians formed the largest group of immigrants. Austrians, Czechs, Hungarians, and Slovaks were the next biggest group. Also notable within this wave were the Eastern European Jews and the Polish. Many of the Jews left their homelands because of religious persecution.

Just as the immigrants had many different reasons for coming to America, they had many different experiences here, too. Many immigrants were poor. They were forced to work as unskilled laborers. They worked on ships and built roads. They worked on the railroads and in the factories. They did all types of hard work. Others saved their money to buy shops where they used the different skills brought from their homelands. Though the work was hard and often low paying, immigrants—especially of the second wave—were able to find jobs. The country's growth, particularly in cities like New York, demanded cheap labor.

States had their own immigration laws until the late 1800s. Then the United States government set up immigration laws. In 1892, an immigration center was set up on Ellis Island in New York Harbor. All immigrants had to stop there first. At Ellis Island, the immigrants waited in line to be examined by doctors. If they passed inspection, the immigrants were issued a card that allowed them to enter the United States. Because of the thousands of people streaming through the immigration centers daily, the process was often hurried. Sometimes, if a person's name was hard to spell, the official making out the card would simplify it. A name like *Smolinski* might have been changed to *Smith*.

The Statue of Liberty

Once their ships sailed into the harbor, the immigrants looked eagerly for the Statue of Liberty. This statue was a gift from the French people to the American people. It was meant to

To many immigrants sailing into New York Harbor, the Statue of Liberty was a symbol of hope for a better life.

New York Convention & Visitors Bureau

honor the American spirit of freedom and had been placed in the harbor as a symbol of that freedom. The statue bears a famous message of welcome to immigrants. The message—a poem titled "The New Colossus" by Emma Lazarus—is found on a plaque on the statue's pedestal. It reads, in part:

. . . Give me your tired, your poor, Your huddled masses yearning to breathe free. . . .

The statue was built by Frederic Auguste Bartholdi, a Frenchman. With donations from the American people, a pedestal for the statue was built. Even children donated money. One young girl, for example, offered to sell a pair of pet chickens to help raise the money. The statue was built in France and shipped in pieces to the United States. It took seventeen railroad cars to carry the crates to the shipping docks in France. The statue was unveiled in New York Harbor in 1886.

By 1980, the statue was in need of repair. Through the early 1980s, the American people worked hard to restore the statue to its original beauty. The shiny, like-new statue became the center of Bicentennial celebrations that marked the two-hundred-year anniversary of the United States. A special celebration was held in October 1986 to mark the statue's centennial.

It is interesting to note that the small island that holds the statue, Liberty Island, is actually part of New Jersey. The statue can be seen from New York, and it lies in New York Harbor, but the Statue of Liberty is actually in New Jersey.

Sophia—One Immigrant's Story

Sophia, a woman who emigrated from Russia in 1904 when she was five, remembers what it was like:

My father had already gone to America and worked for an elevator company. When my mother got word that he had been killed in an accident, she decided to go to America to see if it was true. We of course traveled in steerage [the lower levels of the ship]. I thought that was how everyone traveled. I did not realize the wealthy ones on deck traveled in comfort.

All of our belongings were kept in our bunks, including salami and other foods. Everyone else had smelly food, too. The food attracted bugs and lice. The lice got into everyone's hair. The itching was awful.

We arrived at Ellis Island at night. There were shouts of joy when we saw the lights of the Statue of Liberty.

At Ellis Island, Sophia's mother was told she could not enter the country because she had an eye disease. There was no ship going to Russia, so the family was sent to Paris. Eventually they returned to Russia, hitchhiking much of the way.

Two years later, Sophia's mother made a second voyage to the United States. Sophia and her sister stayed in Russia with their grandparents. The sisters made the trip two years later with relatives. They managed to get an eighth-grade education before going to work at age fourteen. They continued their education in night school.

Immigration Slows

The number of immigrants entering this country slowed down after 1914. Strict immigration laws passed after World War I restricted the total number of immigrants to 150,000 per year. The laws also determined from where these immigrants came by setting a limit on the number of immigrants from individual countries. The individual limits were based on the number of people from that country already living in the United States in 1920. This policy, called the national-origins system, favored immigrants from northern and western Europe.

The Great Depression began in 1929. During the depression there weren't many jobs, and farming was poor. Not as many foreigners wanted to come to this country, even though the depression hit most countries around the world.

But two groups of people did continue coming: the Jews and the Puerto Ricans. In the mid-1900s, many Jewish people came to America. These immigrants came because Adolf Hitler, who persecuted the Jews, rose to power in Germany. Europe was in chaos with World War II, which lasted from 1939-1945. Today, more than two million Jews live in New York City.

A second group, the Puerto Ricans, also continued coming to America in the 1930s. Living and working conditions in Puerto Rico were poor, and they wanted a new life in America. Many settled in New York, but they soon found they were not welcome in many neighborhoods. So many Puerto Ricans settled on the eastern fringes of Harlem. The area became known as Spanish Harlem. By the late 1940s, the Spanish-speaking population in New York numbered over half a million people.

In November of 1954, the immigration center on Ellis Island was closed. It had operated for sixty-two years. In that time, twenty million immigrants had stopped at Ellis Island.

New York Is Rich in Cultures

The United States is sometimes called the "melting pot" of the world. This is because so many foreign people came to this country and blended in with each other. They worked and lived with people from different lands. They married each other and had children. This has happened to an extent in New York City. But New York, like the rest of the country, is also a place where people enjoy keeping their national heritage. New York is more like a salad bowl than a melting pot. In a salad bowl, all the ingredients keep their identities, but together they make a better salad than each ingredient would alone.

Each group of immigrants has had an impact on the city. New York City is a rich blend of cultures because of this. But it is also a city with separate ethnic neighborhoods. Many blacks and Puerto Ricans live in Harlem. A section called Woodside is home to many Greeks. Little Italy is known for its Italian population, and many Chinese live in Chinatown.

Scheduled to open in 1990 as an immigration museum, Ellis Island is being restored with funds raised by the Statue of Liberty-Ellis Island Foundation.

© Peter B. Kaplan, 1982

In Manhattan, you can see and experience the blend of cultures. If you get on a bus, you will see many different people. The bus driver might be from Pakistan. The police officer directing traffic may be Irish. Many of the signs on the bus are written in English and Spanish. The bus may pass by a Greek Orthodox church, a Jewish synagogue, and a Buddhist temple. Once off the bus, you can buy ethnic foods at various stands and restaurants: Jewish bagels, French pastries, Swiss chocolates, Chinese egg rolls, or Mexican burritos.

Religion

Religious freedom was one of the biggest reasons people came to the New World. This is noticeable in New York even today—it is a city of many churches and many different faiths. People belonging to most of the world's major religions can be found in the city. Some of the world's most famous churches are in Manhattan. St. Patrick's Cathedral is a very large and beautiful Gothic cathedral on Fifth Avenue. Construction began on St. Patrick's in 1858. The Episcopal Cathedral of St. John the Divine, on the northwest side of Manhattan, is the largest Gothic cathedral in the world. Temple Emanu-El was founded in 1845 and is the oldest Jewish Reform Congregation in New York. It is located on the west side of Central Park.

Carlye Calvin

Built in the style of Europe's gothic churches, St. Patrick's Cathedral rises more than 300 feet (91 m) above busy Fifth Avenue.

WORLD CITIES

Places in the City

If you visit New York City, the first things you will notice are the skyscrapers. Manhattan is perfect for these towering buildings because it is a small island made of rock. The island and its skyscrapers are a center for transportation, commerce, and entertainment. Manhattan is the heart of New York City.

A City of Skyscrapers

There are many historic and wondrous skyscrapers to see in Manhattan. The tallest are the twin towers that make up the World Trade Center. These skyscrapers stretch nearly a quarter of a mile into the sky. From the Rooftop Promenade on the 110th floor of one of the towers, you can enjoy a 55-mile (88 km) view. When you stroll the Rooftop Promenade, you're walking on the world's highest outdoor observatory platform.

When workers dug the foundation for the World Trade Center, they dumped the dirt in the Hudson River. This dirt added another 23.5 acres (9.5 hectares) to Battery Park. This park, at the southernmost tip of Manhattan, was restored in 1912. From the park, visitors can catch a ferry that takes them to the Statue of Liberty and Ellis Island.

In the middle of Manhattan—called Midtown Manhattan—stands the Empire State Building. For many years, the Empire State Building was the giant of the city. At 102 stories and

The Chrysler Building, with its well-known spire, juts above the Manhattan skyline.

1,250 feet (381 m) high, it was the tallest building in the world when it was completed in 1931. The Chrysler Building is another famous skyscraper. Its unusual spire, lit at night, is a familiar part of the night skyline.

Many skyscrapers built in the 1930s make up the area known as Rockefeller Center. Radio City Music Hall and the headquarters for the Radio Corporation of America (RCA) and the National Broadcasting Company (NBC) are located in the area. Shops, restaurants, and a skating rink are found in the center of Rockefeller Center.

Historic Places in the City

You can walk from the World Trade Center to many famous and historic places. You can visit Wall Street, the world's center of finance. Wall Street is short, narrow, and curvy. High-rise buildings line the sides of the street. Traveling down Wall Street is like adventuring through a canyon, with high cliffs all around. Watch out for the Wall Street messengers riding bicycles. They move very fast and dart in and out of traffic.

From the World Trade Center, you can also walk to Federal Hall, where George Washington was sworn in as the first president of the United States. North from there is Fulton Street, with its lively (and smelly) fish market. East of Fulton Street is the South Street Seaport. Here you'll see a museum filled with mementos of nineteenth century shipping days. Old seaport buildings have been restored to the way they looked in 1800. And at the docks you'll see historic sailing ships. You'll probably want to see Castle Clinton on the southernmost point of Manhattan in Battery Park. It was once a fort and later became the first immigration center.

Neighborhoods of New York

Manhattan's ethnic neighborhoods are favorites with tourists and New Yorkers alike. You can buy fortune cookies in colorful Chinatown. You can make a phone call from a Chinese-style phone booth. Or, you can try the pizza in Little Italy. In New York, people buy pizza by the slice and roll it up to eat it. In Greenwich Village's Washington Square, you'll see people playing boccie, an old Italian sport similar to bowling.

Many Jewish merchants sell their goods on the Lower East Side. On Sundays, the streets there are closed to traffic and used just for street vendors and shoppers. Harlem, on the north side, is rich with black culture and tradition. Harlem's world-famous Apollo Theater presents great performers. Recently, the neighborhood called Soho (for "South of Houston Street") has become a special area of artists' studios, galleries, and craft shops.

You'll want to visit Central Park, too. One way to see the park is to take a ride in a horse-drawn carriage called a hansom cab. On pleasant weekends, many cyclists, joggers, and walkers enjoy the park. In the winter, people ice skate on the ponds.

Museums and More Fun

In Central Park, you'll also find the famous Metropolitan Museum of Art. Both adults and children enjoy the Junior Museum wing. Favorite attractions are the ancient Egyptian and Oriental collections.

New York State Economic Development

Radio City Music Hall features daily performances by its famous dance troupe, the Rockettes.

Other museums you may want to see are the American Museum of Natural History, the Museum of Modern Art, the Guggenheim Museum, the Whitney Museum of American Art, the American Museum of Immigration, the Museum of the American Indian, and the Guinness World Records Exhibit Hall. Touring the museums is an education in itself.

You can see wonderful shows and sports events at Madison Square Garden. There is top entertainment at Radio City Music Hall. The New York Metropolitan Opera is world-famous. Carnegie Hall is newly restored. The world's most prestigious singers and musicians perform there. The Lincoln Center for the Performing Arts consists of six stone-and-glass buildings on Broadway. Music,

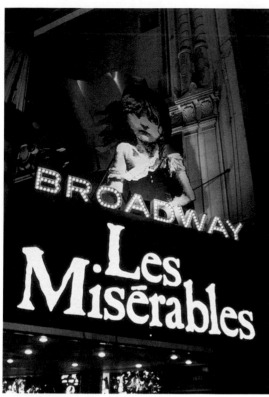

Brightly lit marquees like this one have earned Broadway its nickname, "The Great White Way."

dance, and theater groups perform in the center's three main theaters. Don't miss Broadway and Times Square either. Broadway, in the Times Square area, provides this country with its most grand theater. In the evening, Broadway is nicknamed "The Great White Way" because of all the bright white lights that light up the theaters. No other city can quite match the excitement felt here, especially on theater opening nights. It was here that a special type of theater was developed that has remained very popular—the Broadway musical. In other sections of the city there is a wonderful tradition of theater called "Off-Broadway."

The Times Square area of New York was renamed in 1904 after the *New York Times* newspaper built its tower there. The *Times* moved into its new building on New Year's Eve and celebrated with a fireworks display at midnight. This began a tradition that continues today. The celebration can be seen on television from anywhere in the country.

A Year in New York

New York has special events throughout the year. In January, huge paper dragons parade through Chinatown in celebration of the Chinese New Year. On St. Patrick's Day, it seems that everyone is Irish. New York City has a bigger St. Patrick's Day parade than Dublin, Ireland has.

In April, Fifth Avenue is filled with Greeks in native costume for the Greek Day Parade. Fifth Avenue is again filled with the sounds of celebration in May, when New Yorkers turn out for the Martin Luther King Memorial Day Parade. In June, it's the Puerto Rican Day Parade. The Italian Street Festival in "Little Italy" is held in July. The Italians also celebrate the

Feast of San Gennaro there.

In August, you can hear the thunderous sound of several thousand tapping feet taking part in Macy's Parade of Tap Dancers. In November, you can watch the difficult finish of the New York City Marathon in Central Park. You have probably seen Macy's Thanksgiving Day Parade on television. It's even more fun to watch in person.

In December, New York glows with the red, green, and white lights of Christmas. Holiday windows on Fifth Avenue are spectacular. The streets are closed on the Sundays before Christmas so people can walk along and enjoy the decorated windows. On New Year's Eve, crowds of people gather in Times Square to ring in the New Year.

Any time is the right time to visit New York.

A procession of colossal balloon figures is a highlight of Macy's Thanksgiving Day Parade.

New York State Commerce Department

WORLD CITIES

New York's Boroughs

If you look again at a map of New York, you will be reminded of how the land is broken up by waterways. It is these natural features that divide New York into its natural regions. A native New Yorker rarely says he or she is from New York City. Instead, New Yorkers say they are from Staten Island or Brooklyn or one of the other three boroughs. Each borough has its own government, headed by a borough president. The mayor of New York City is in charge over all the boroughs. Each borough has a unique character and special attractions.

Manhattan

The island of Manhattan is the center of New York City. It contains the central business district, the financial center, and the major shopping and theater districts. The island of Manhattan is surrounded by the Hudson River, the Harlem River, the East River, and New York Bay. A small part of the borough is on the mainland to the north.

Since the other boroughs are separated from Manhattan by water, people had to devise ways to get to Manhattan. Ferry boats could not carry all of the people who needed to travel back and forth. But when bridges were constructed—especially the Brooklyn Bridge in 1883, the Triborough Bridge in 1936, and the Verrazano-Narrows Bridge in 1964—the boroughs became linked to Manhattan.

Brooklyn

Across the bay from the lower tip of Manhattan is Brooklyn. It was the first of the boroughs to be connected by a bridge to Manhattan. Brooklyn is a mixture of both small shops and many homes. Brooklyn neighborhoods range from well-kept ones such as those in Brooklyn Heights, America's first suburb, to ones that are run down such as those in Bedford-Stuyvesant. The Dutch influence has lasted longer in Brooklyn than in the other boroughs. Many Brooklyn natives, like many of the Dutch, show an adventurous spirit about business and about life. The borough was first called Bruekelen, after a village in Holland. Local landmarks also show the Dutch influence, and many old buildings are in the Dutch colonial style.

In addition to the Dutch influence, the communities of Jewish people, Italians, and Mohawk Indians influence the life and look of Brooklyn, as well as all of New York City. Many of the footpaths of the Mohawks became major streets.

Major attractions in Brooklyn are Coney Island and the Botanic Gardens. Although Coney Island no longer boasts the many amusements of its past, its beaches are still very popular. Part of a wonderful park, the lush and peaceful Botanic Garden provides relief from the bustle of the city.

Queens

North and east of Brooklyn is Queens. John F. Kennedy International Airport and La Guardia Airport are located here. Queens has rows and rows of private homes and many large apartment buildings. There are communities of Irish, Italians, and Greeks. Queens has more parks than any other borough has.

A special attraction in Queens is the Jamaica Bay Wildlife Refuge. It has more than three hundred species of birds and an excellent view of the New York skyline. Queens forms the northwestern tip of Long Island, a wooded island with long beaches and many homes. Long Island is indeed long—it extends about 120 miles (193 km) east from the mouth of the Hudson River into the Atlantic Ocean. The borough of Brooklyn lies partly in Long Island.

The Brooklyn Bridge spans the East River to link Manhattan with its sister borough of Brooklyn.

New York Convention & Visitors Bureau

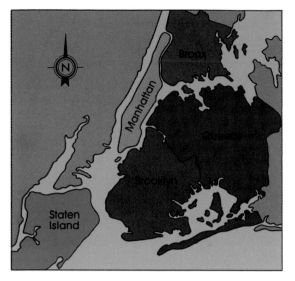

This map shows the city's five boroughs.

The Bronx

North and east of Manhattan is the Bronx. It is the only borough that lies on the United States mainland. In the Bronx are several streets lined with five- and six-story apartment buildings. There are also many private homes. Many Puerto Ricans and other people from the Caribbean islands now live in the Bronx.

Yankee Stadium, the Bronx Zoo, and Van Cortland Park are the borough's main attractions. The zoo can be toured on a monorail. An interesting feature of the zoo is that animals are housed in natural settings, not in cages.

Staten Island

Staten Island is the only borough not directly linked to Manhattan. It lies between the southern tip of Manhattan and New Jersey. It is connected to Brooklyn by the Verrazano-Narrows Bridge. Before this bridge was built in 1964, Staten Island was a rural island. Once the bridge was completed, however, people living on this island had easy access to jobs in the city. Many more people began to move to Staten Island, and today it is a growing suburb. It attracts people who want to escape more crowded parts of the city. Yet, many of the island's woods and meadows are now disappearing because of the island's population growth.

The Staten Island Historical Society Museum has restored some pre-revolutionary buildings. One of these is the oldest elementary schoolhouse in the United States. Another attraction is the Staten Island Ferry. A ride on the ferry offers a good view of the Statue of Liberty and Ellis Island. Best of all, the ferry is cheap; it costs twenty-five cents round trip.

New York Islands and Waterways

In addition to the five boroughs, over fifty small islands dot New York waterways. Only a few have people living on them today. Many of the islands have colorful histories. Immigrants who did not pass health examinations were kept on Hoffman Island

Brooklyn's Coney Island, with its carnival atmosphere, gives its visitors a brief escape from everyday life.

and Swiburne Island in New York Harbor. Today, both islands are wildlife refuges—places that shelter animals. Roosevelt Island, also in New York Harbor, was formerly called Welfare Island. It had a charity hospital, a prison, a poorhouse, and a mental hospital. Today, Roosevelt Island is a thriving community. The island's residents are proud of the clean streets, good schools, and low crime rate.

Water, more than any other feature, defines the areas of New York City. Wherever you are in the city, you are never far from water—the Atlantic Ocean, New York Bay, the Harlem River, the East River, and the Hudson River. These waterways form the natural boundaries of the boroughs. But most importantly, these waterways have made New York the busiest shipping port in the nation.

WORLD

CITIES

What Makes New York Work?

Cities thrive on trade. A city's location and resources play important roles in developing its trade. A city needs to receive goods from other places and to sell goods to other places. Therefore, its location is very important. The transportation systems—the waterways, railroads, and highways—are important to a city. Natural resources, such as water and fertile land, are important, too.

But New York's major resource is its people. People are sometimes called human resources. Think of New York's human resources as all the various New Yorkers working together to make their city great. The city must also take care of its people. Cities provide jobs for people, places for them to shop, and public services such as transportation, schools, libraries, police and fire protection, and garbage collection.

Remember, New York is located on the Atlantic Ocean and is surrounded by deep rivers. Because of this location and these natural features, New York grew as a colony and continued to grow as an American city. It became the busiest shipping port in the nation —shipping goods to and receiving goods from countries all over the world. Many of the things you use every day were shipped to New York City before they were transported to wherever you live.

New York City is the center for finance in the nation and the world.

Many banks and brokerage offices are located here. Many people work in New York's financial businesses. Financial decisions made here affect the economy all over the nation.

Major publishers of books, magazines, and newspapers are located in New York. Famous advertising agencies are also located here. Many of the commercials seen on television are created by New York companies. Most of the major television networks are located in New York. Thus, the city attracts many writers, actors, and journalists.

New York City is a major research center, containing some of the world's great libraries and museums. It is the home of Columbia University, an academic center known around the world. Thousands of New Yorkers attend the many branches of the City University of New York.

Small Manufacturers and Businesses

Many large corporations have their headquarters in New York. But it is also a city of many small businesses and shops.

But, unlike many cities, New York is not a major manufacturing center. Most of its factories are small, each employing an average of thirty people. The major manufactured item is clothing. The garment industry began dur-

This monument, found in Manhattan's garment district, honors the workers whose labors built the New York clothing industry.

ing the Civil War, when small groups of tailors made uniforms for the soldiers. As the industry grew, people learned a method of mass producing uniforms. Soon all types of clothes or garments were mass produced.

Transporting People

Many more people work in New York City than live there. People who come into the city just to work are called commuters. They commute from many places in New York State and from the neighboring states of New Jersey, Connecticut, and Pennsylvania. They commute by private cars and by public transportation—train, bus, or subway. The people who use public transportation daily within the city number approximately 850,000. Dur-

New Yorkers use crowded, noisy subway cars for the daily ride to and from work.

ing workdays, many trains come into Grand Central Station carrying thousands of commuters. Grand Central Station is one of the largest train stations in the country—and one of the busiest. It has two levels of tracks to handle over 550 scheduled train trips each day.

The city is able to manage so many people in such a small area because of its skyscrapers, transportation systems, and city planning. In addition to a network of trains coming into and leaving the city each day, the city has a vast subway system. Subways are the main people movers within the city. More than one billion people ride the subway each year. Separate subway systems in New York were built in the early 1900s and joined together in the late 1930s. Today, the subway system covers a route of over 200 miles (322 km). It is a crowded means of public transportation, but it works.

John Randel developed the city's street plan in 1811. It was a practical plan for organizing the city's buildings and transporting people. Many cities today use this same street plan. Randel's design consists of rows and rows of straight streets crossing each other at right angles to form a "grid." Streets run in an east-west direction and avenues run north and south. Most streets and avenues are numbered, rather than named, to make it easy to find an address. For example, it is *easy* to find Fifth Avenue. Just find any other numbered avenue, and start counting. (From Fourth Avenue, for example, travel just one block to Fifth Avenue.)

New York's Planning Commission tried to extend Randel's plan as the city grew. Although the plan is a good one, driving a car is frustrating in New York City today. (Parking a car can be almost impossible.) The streets are crowded, and traffic moves slowly. Traffic engineers have tried to solve the city's traffic jams by closing certain streets to cars during certain times of the day. People can also use the city's buses. For door-to-door service, there are the famous New York City taxicabs. New York City has over twelve thousand cabs. Bridges, of course, provide an important link for transporta-

The New York Stock Exchange (below) and the rest of Wall Street cover an area that developed before a street plan for the city was designed.

tion between the various boroughs of the city. One fun transportation link is the Staten Island Ferry. Some people ride the ferry to and from their jobs or homes on Staten Island each day.

New York Is for People

People enjoy cultural events, and New York offers more of them than any other city in the United States. New York's great museums and Broad-way theaters attract both tourists and New Yorkers. Because New York is a center for entertainment—with its many theaters, concert halls, and entertainment complexes—New York is as lively a city at night as it is during the day. Many restaurants and night-clubs stay open until three or four o'clock in the morning. Some stay open all night.

People also enjoy sporting events.

The twenty thousand-seat Madison Square Garden provides a center for convention groups and sporting events.

New York Convention & Visitors Bureau

Madison Square Garden in Manhattan is the center for sports activities. The sports area was built in 1925. Boxing, hockey, and basketball events are held there. Other sports events such as ice skating and national horse shows are held there, too. Besides the sports arena, Madison Square Garden is home to an exposition center, an art gallery, a cinema, bowling alleys, and restaurants.

Yankee Stadium, the home of the New York Yankees baseball team, is in the Bronx. The stadium was built in 1922. During the 1920s, New York Yankee Babe Ruth became famous for hitting many home runs. So many people came to see him play baseball that Yankee Stadium, which opened in 1923, is often called "the House that Ruth Built." Shea Stadium is in Queens. Both the New York Mets baseball team and the New York Jets football team play in Shea Stadium. The 200-acre (81 ha) Aqueduct horse-racing track is also located in Queens. Forest Hills and Flushing Meadow tennis clubs in Queens are well known in the tennis world.

Shopping in New York City is an event in itself. Since the mid-1900s, New York has been one of the best places in the world to shop. From the early days of the garment-making industry, New York has been a center for design and fashion. The most famous stores are located on or near Fifth Avenue. Some of these stores are Lord and Taylor, Saks Fifth Avenue, and Tiffany's. The city also is the home of many famous department stores, such as Macy's and Bloomingdale's. Throughout the city, in the different ethnic neighborhoods, specialty shops offer good bargains.

Adventures in New York

There is an excitement about New York. People complain that it is dirty, crowded, and dangerous, but New Yorkers say they love the feeling of excitement. This excitement, many say, can be found in no other city in the world. New York is an adventure, which Helen Keller, the deaf and blind lecturer and writer, described with these words:

Tremulously I stand in the subways. Fearful, I touch the forest of steel girders aloud with the thunder of oncoming trains that shoot past me like projectiles. Another train bursts into the station like a volcano, the people crowd me on. In a few minutes, still trembling, I am spilled into the streets.

WORLD CITIES

New York in the World

New York City plays an important role both in the United States and in the world. It is a world center for shipping, finance, business, theater, the arts, television, publishing, and tourism.

A Busy Shipping Center

From the days of the fur traders, New York has been a lively shipping port. In the early days, beaver pelts were sent to Holland, and goods needed to build the new colony were brought from Europe.

The opening of the Erie Canal in 1825 was an important link to the western frontier. The canal ran from the city of Buffalo on Lake Erie to the city of Albany on the Hudson River.

The Erie Canal made it much easier and less expensive to transport goods to other parts of the country. Today, however, most goods are not shipped on the canal. Instead, most goods are carried in and out of New York by truck and train.

An Important Financial Center

New York City has been the country's center of finance since the Revolutionary War. What happens on Wall Street affects the economy of the country and the rest of the world. You may remember the stock market crash on October 19, 1987. You may even know someone who lost money in the crash. It happened on Wall Street in

New York, and it affected the entire world.

Many very large companies have their headquarters, or main office, in New York City. Decisions that are made at these headquarters affect employees in branch offices all over the world. These decisions also affect other companies selling the same kind of product.

An Exciting Entertainment Center

New York City is known throughout the world for its theater productions both on and off Broadway. The Metropolitan Museum of Art is also world famous. Productions that are filmed in New York's major television studios may be seen around the world. The headquarters for the three major television networks—ABC, CBS Inc., and NBC—are in New York City.

Many of the world's largest publishers also have their offices in New York City. New York City book publishers include Doubleday, Random House, and Simon & Schuster. Time-Life, Conde-Nast, and Hearst are large magazine publishing companies. Many music publishing companies also are headquartered there.

New York and the World

In 1939 and 1940, New York hosted the New York World's Fair in Flush-ing Meadow, a section of Queens. In 1964 and 1965, New York hosted another world's fair on the same site. This fair had more than 150 large exhibit halls. The theme for the fair was "Peace Through Understanding."

Just how important New York is to the rest of the world can be seen in one group of buildings—the United Nations headquarters. New York is the home of the United Nations, which is an organization of more than 150 nations from around the world. It was organized during the 1940s after World War II to help keep world peace and security. Representatives from the

The soaring lines of the United Nations headquarters mirror the organization's hope for world peace.

Carlye Calvin

Carlye Calvin

member nations meet in the United Nation's buildings that are found along the East River. These buildings were dedicated in 1952.

To handle the many businesspeople, tourists, and residents, New York City needs three major airports. John F. Kennedy International Airport is the eastern hub for international travel. La Guardia Airport is in Queens, and Newark International Airport is in nearby New Jersey. People from all over the world enter the United States by way of New York. As in the past, some people stay, while others travel on to different cities. But New York is their introduction to the United States, just as it was for the immigrants many years ago.

New York in the Future

New York City is like a magnet. It attracts many people seeking careers

New York's people are the force that will determine the city's future.

in art, theater, television, journalism, writing, banking and finance, and fashion. Most likely, New York will continue to survive because it will be able to answer the needs of the country and the world. As the United States advances in technology and communications, more and more people will work in these fields. The resource for the future is talented people. The people of New York City are a very special resource.

As you leave New York City after a visit, you will take with you many thoughts about the "Big Apple." You will always remember the towering skyscrapers, the noise of the traffic, and the many different people. You will also remember a city rich in history and an energy as great as that in any other city in the world.

New York City: Historical Events

1524 Giovanni da Verrazano sails into New York Bay.

1609 Henry Hudson establishes the settlement of New Netherland.

1626 Peter Minuit purchases Manhattan Island from the Indians.

1664 Great Britain claims "New York" as a colony.

1689 The first mayor, Peter Delanoy, is elected.

1723 New York's population reaches 7,248.

1735 John Peter Zenger, publisher of *New-York Weekly Journal,* is found innocent of a libel charge. The case becomes an important milestone for freedom of the press.

1774 The Sons of Liberty hold a "tea party" to protest high taxes.

1785-1790 New York City serves as the capital of the United States.

1789 George Washington takes oath in New York City as the first president of the United States.

1817 Work begins on the Erie Canal. This waterway, which connects the Hudson River with Lake Erie and all of the Great Lakes, opens in 1825.

1835 The Great Fire destroys much of the city.

1863 Mobs riot in opposition to the Union Army draft for the Civil War.

1877 After twenty years of work, Central Park opens in the middle of Manhattan.

1878 The first elevated railroad is built.

1883 The Brooklyn Bridge is completed. Manhattan is now directly connected to Brooklyn.

1886 The Statue of Liberty is unveiled in New York Harbor.

1892 Ellis Island opens as an immigration center.

1898 Greater New York is formed.

1902 The Metropolitan Museum of Art is founded.

1922 Yankee Stadium is built.

1925 Madison Square Garden is built.

1929 The Museum of Modern Art is founded.

Wall Street's stock market crashes. The Great Depression follows, hitting New York City hard.

1931 At its opening, the Empire State Building is the world's tallest building.

1934 Fiorello La Guardia becomes mayor.

1939 La Guardia Airport, named for the popular mayor, opens.

1939-1940 New York City is the site of the World's Fair.

1952 The United Nations headquarters is established in the city.

1964-1965 New York City is again the site of the World's Fair.

1977 Ed Koch becomes mayor.

1987 The stock market crashes again but eventually recovers.

New York City

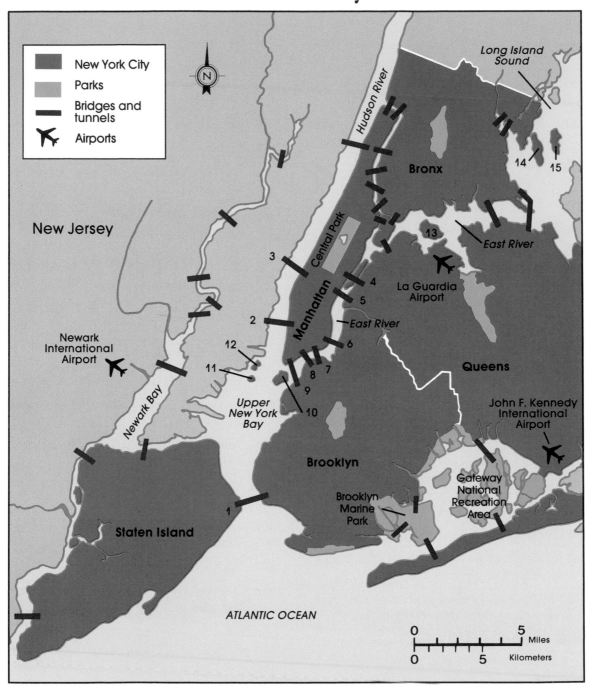

Legend:
- New York City
- Parks
- Bridges and tunnels
- ✈ Airports

New Jersey

Long Island Sound

Hudson River

Bronx

14   15

Central Park

13

East River

La Guardia Airport

3

Manhattan

4

5

East River

Queens

2

12

6

Newark International Airport

11

8   7

9

Upper New York Bay

10

John F. Kennedy International Airport

Newark Bay

Brooklyn

Gateway National Recreation Area

Brooklyn Marine Park

Staten Island

1

ATLANTIC OCEAN

0   5 Miles

0   5 Kilometers

Map Key

1 Verrazano-Narrows Bridge	6 Williamsburg Bridge	11 Statue of Liberty
2 Holland Tunnel	7 Manhattan Bridge	12 Ellis Island
3 Lincoln Tunnel	8 Brooklyn Bridge	13 Rikers Island
4 Queensboro Bridge	9 Brooklyn Battery Tunnel	14 City Island
5 Queens-Midtown Tunnel	10 Governors Island	15 Hart Island

New York City Almanac

Location: Latitude—40.4° north. Longitude—73.6° west.

Climate: Temperate—warm summers and cold, damp winters. Average January temperature—32°F (0°C). Average July temperature—77°F (25°C). Average annual precipitation—40 inches (102 cm). Average annual snowfall—30 inches (76 cm).

Land Area: TOTAL: 300 sq. miles (777 sq. km). Manhattan—23 sq. miles (60 sq. km). Bronx—41 sq. miles (106 sq. km). Staten Island—58 sq. miles (150 sq. km). Brooklyn—70 sq. miles (181 sq. km). Queens—108 sq. miles (280 sq. km).

Population: 7,071,639 people (1980 census). World ranking—7. Population density—23,455 persons/sq. mile.

Major Airports: John F. Kennedy International Airport, La Guardia Airport, and Newark Airport (New Jersey). A total of 27 million passengers depart from these airports per year.

Colleges/Universities: 120 colleges, universities, and other institutions of higher learning, including Columbia University, City University of New York, New York University, Fordham University, and Juilliard School of Music.

Media: Newspapers—main newspapers are *The New York Times, Wall Street Journal, New York Post, Daily News*. Radio—29 licensed AM/FM stations. Television—headquarters for the three major national television networks: National Broadcasting Company (NBC), Columbia Broadcasting System (CBS), and American Broadcasting Company (ABC).

Major Buildings: Citicorp Center—46 stories, 914 feet (278 m). Chrysler Building—77 stories, 1,046 feet (319 m). Empire State Building—102 stories, 1,250 feet (381 m). World Trade Center—110 stories, 1,350 feet (411 m).

Port: Port of New York and New Jersey—166,991,220 tons/year.

Tunnels: Four rapid transit tunnels (Hudson River Tunnels), Queens Midtown Tunnel, Brooklyn-Battery Tunnel, Lincoln Tunnel, Holland Tunnel.

Bridges: 62 major bridges, including Brooklyn Bridge, George Washington Bridge, Triborough Bridge, Manhattan Bridge, Bayonne Bridge, and Verrazano-Narrows Bridge.

Interesting Facts: The nation's first patent was issued in New York City on July 31, 1790, to Samuel Hopkins for a process involved in soap making.

The nation's first strike on union record was by the Journeymen Printers in 1776 in New York City.

Index

DATE DUE			
MAR 1 2 2000			
MAR 1 4 2000			
FEB 0 7			
APR 2 1			